Light Meals
Including
Cold Dishes and
Outdoor Cooking

Published by
Octopus Books Pty. Ltd.,
30 Corben Street,
Surry Hills,
New South Wales, 2010

First published 1971
© Copyright Octopus Books Pty.
Ltd. 1971. Printed in Hong Kong
by Lee Fung Printing Co. Ltd.
Distributed to the Trade by
Crescent Books
L468
ILLUSTRATION/MURRAY ZANONI

Light Meals
Including Cold Dishes and Outdoor Cooking

Kim MacDonald

Crescent Books

Preface

It is necessary to eat special foods in a hot climate.
Chilled food is both nourishing and cooling. Surprisingly,
hot, spicy food has the same effect.
Cool, refreshing, tasty dishes should be served in hot,
humid weather or in the middle of a heatwave in order
to stimulate jaded palates and to refresh and feed the
body.
In this book you will find a variety of simple-to-follow
recipes for dishes to serve in a hot climate. Hot weather
catering for the family and friends will no longer be a
problem if you use the ideas in this practical cookery book.

The Editor would like to acknowledge and thank the
following for their kind assistance in providing
props for the photographs in this book.
Incorporated Agencies Pty. Ltd., Sydney
Ban Kura Gift Shop, Cremorne Centre, Cremorne, Sydney
Suomi, Double Bay, Sydney
The Bay Tree, Woollahra, Sydney
Dry Red, 429 Liverpoool Street, Darlinghurst

Contents

Weights and Measures

All measurements are given in cups, tablespoons and teaspoons.

1 standard measuring cup 8 fl oz
1 standard measuring tablespoon 20 ml
1 standard measuring teaspoon 5 ml

Australian, American and Canadian measures are the same, with one exception. The North American tablespoon measures 15 ml. Therefore, American and Canadian readers should add a teaspoon measure to every tablespoon required.
All measurements given are level.
To level a cup measure, shake the cup gently and check the measurements at eye level.
For an accurate spoon measure, level the ingredients off with the back of a palette, French or kitchen knife or with the back of a spatula.

Note In Australia 2½ cups liquid = 20 fl oz = 1 pint
In America & Canada 2 cups liquid = 16 fl oz = 1 pint

In Australia, the Imperial pint of 20 fluid ounces is used (as in Britain), but in America and Canada the 16 fluid ounce pint is used. To avoid confusion, all liquid measurements used in the recipes in this book are given in the 8 fluid ounce cup.

Oven Temperature Guide

Description of Oven	Automatic Electric °F.	Gas °F.
Cool	200	200
Very Slow	250	250
Slow	300–325	300
Moderately Slow	325–350	325
Moderate	350–375	350
Moderately Hot	375–400	375
Hot	400–450	400
Very Hot	450–500	450

Introduction

Here is a recipe book you will love to use if you
live in a hot climate or if you have to cope with a
heatwave.
This book gives you ideas for The First Course, The
Main Course, Salads, Desserts and Cool Drinks; ideas
for feeding family and friends throughout a long, hot
summer.
Refreshing ingredients are used in many of the recipes
to sharpen appetites, and contrasting flavours enliven
the taste buds.
Lime juice or lemon juice may be used in dressings for
salads and hors d'oeuvre, in savoury dishes, desserts and
cool drinks.
Other citrus fruit such as oranges and grapefruit and
juicy tropical fruits such as mangoes, pawpaws and
pineapples are served in hors d'oeuvre, salads, desserts
and drinks.
Natural yoghurt with its tangy flavour is used when
making hors d'oeuvre, soups, salads and desserts.
Cool vegetables, salad plants and fruits which are high
in water content are used in many of the recipes; these
include cucumbers, melons, lettuce, radishes, tomatoes
and salad greens.
Use is made of spices, hot chillis, coconut milk,
coconut cream and soy sauce in curries and barbecues
and in some salads. These ingredients add to the flavour,
but also play an important role in cooling the body and
replacing lost natural salt and moisture.
I have tried to keep the cook-housewife in mind when
planning this book by including recipes which require
little or no cooking. Naturally, some of The Main Course
dishes have to be cooked, but these can be prepared in
the cool of the evening, and they require very little
attention during cooking.

Again, in The Dessert Course chapter the only cooking required
is to thicken a custard or dissolve some gelatine. So
you can keep your kitchen as cool as possible with these
recipe ideas, which is most important in summer weather.
All the recipes are easy to follow and the dishes
are simple to make and serve. Food for a hot climate
requires very little garnishing or decoration, but it
should be neatly served and look crisp, appetizing
and refreshing.
With a little thought, planning and organisation, most
of your family's meals may be prepared in advance in
hot weather. I suggest you prepare as much as possible
late at night or early in the morning when the temperature
is cooler, then you too can relax and enjoy the sunshine
in the heat of the day with your family and friends.

The First Course

The First Course, the beginning of the meal, should be small, attractive and appetizing. In hot weather, it should also be very, very cool.

In this chapter I have included recipes for seafood and fruit cocktails, cold fish, vegetable and fruit hors d'oeuvres and chilled spicy soups. These may, in most cases, be prepared well in advance and chilled ready for serving.

An hors d'oeuvre may consist of a single item of food or of a mixture of two, three or more dishes such as pâté with crisp radishes, or slices of hard-boiled egg with dressed zucchini and olives.

Fruit hors d'oeuvres, are particularly good, for they are juicy and refreshing and provide a pleasant introduction to a meal, especially in the heat of a tropical night.

Vegetable hors d'oeuvres are light to eat and have a good flavour and interesting texture. They are usually reasonably inexpensive if you use vegetables in season. Dressed with sharp French dressing or vinaigrette dressing, they are delicious.

Hors d'oeuvres, like salads, should be carefully prepared and arranged neatly and attractively for serving. Many may be served in individual glasses, others on small, individual plates.

The term hors d'oeuvres refers most often to the appetizers served with cocktails before a meal. As these can be fairly substantial, the first course is often omitted.

Many of the recipes in this chapter are best eaten as a first course at the table.

Try home-made tomato juice on a hot night. It is most refreshing and excites the taste buds for the meal to follow. Add ice to each glass before serving to keep it chilled.

Avocado Prawn Cocktail

I have also included some recipes for chilled soups in this chapter. They make an ideal first course in hot weather and are popular with men because they are filling as well as stimulating. Some of them contain spice for this also has a cooling effect. Others contain orange or lemon juice or yoghurt to give a sharp, refreshing flavour.
Try to tempt the palate with some of these attractive, tasty, chilled first courses on hot summer days. If your family or guests enjoy their first course, they are sure to enjoy the rest of the meal.

Avocado Prawn Cocktail

Serves 4

2 avocado pears
8 oz king prawns, peeled
6 tablespoons olive oil
2 tablespoons white wine vinegar
1 tablespoon lemon juice
1 teaspoon sugar
$\frac{1}{4}$ teaspoon dry mustard
$\frac{1}{2}$ teaspoon salt
freshly ground black pepper
$\frac{1}{2}$ tablespoon chopped chives
$\frac{1}{2}$ tablespoon chopped parsley
extra small prawns for garnish

Cut avocado pears in half lengthways and remove stone.
Prepare prawns and place in a bowl.
Place all remaining ingredients, except extra prawns, in a screw-top jar and shake until well mixed. Pour dressing over prawns and leave to stand for 10 minutes.
Serve prawns piled in centre of each avocado pear half.
Serve slightly chilled, garnished with extra small prawns.

Cucumber and Pineapple Hors d'Oeuvre

Serves 6–8

1 small pineapplc
2 small cucumbers
½ cup blanched almonds
½ cup cream
¼ cup lemon juice
salt and peopper

Peel pincapple and cucumber and cut into ½ inch cubes.
Mix with almonds.
Make dressing by mixing cream with lemon juice. Season
to taste with salt and pepper.
Pour dressing over prepared pineapple and cucumber and
serve chilled.
Note: This hors d'oeuvre may also be served as a sambal
(see glossary) with curry.

Florida Cocktail

Serves 6

3 grapefruit
3 large oranges
castor sugar (or powdered sugar)
2 tablespoons kirsch, optional
6 glacé cherries

Peel the grapefruit and oranges with a sharp serrated knife, making sure all the white pith is removed. Cut the fruit into segments and place on a plate. Sprinkle with castor sugar to taste, and kirsch, if desired. Allow to stand at room temperature for 30 minutes.
Arrange the fruit in individual glasses, pour juice over, and decorate with a glacé cherry.
Chill before serving.
Variation: Dry sherry may be used instead of kirsch.

Mushrooms Milord

Serves 4

4 oz green grapes
4 oz button mushrooms
½ cup yoghurt
pinch of sugar

Skin grapes and remove seeds. Wipe mushrooms with a clean, damp cloth and chop finely. Mix grapes and chopped mushrooms with chilled yoghurt and sugar. Chill well. Serve in chilled cocktail glasses.

Grapefruit Shrimp Cocktail

Serves 4

2 grapefruit
4 oz fresh peeled or canned shrimps
3 tablespoons mayonnaise (see page 41)
3 tablespoons whipped cream
1 tablespoon lemon juice
mint leaves for garnish

Cut grapefruit in halves. Using a grapefruit knife or
a small serrated knife remove fruit in neat segments.
Place fruit in a bowl and mix with shrimps.
Carefully remove pith and segment membranes from
grapefruit shells, keeping shells intact.
Mix mayonnaise with whipped cream and lemon juice and
mix with grapefruit segments and shrimps. Place in
grapefruit shells and chill.
Serve cocktail chilled, garnished with mint leaves.
Variation: Small prawns may be used instead of shrimps.

16

Melon
Cocktail

Serves 4

1 small rock or honeydew melon or canteloup
glacé or maraschino cherries
ground or cystallised ginger
castor sugar or powdered sugar

Method 1: Cut melon into quarters lengthways, remove
seeds. Loosen fruit from skin, cut into cubes and reshape
neatly into a wedge on the skin. Decorate each quarter
of melon with a glace or maraschino cherry.
Serve melon chilled with ground ginger and castor sugar.
Method 2: Cut melon into bite-size cubes or into balls
with a melon-ball scoop. Mix melon with 1 tablespoon
chopped crystallized ginger and place in 4 individual
glasses.
Serve chilled with castor sugar.
Variation: Pour a tablespoon of port over each portion
of melon just before serving.

Mushrooms Vinaigrette

Serves 3–4

8 oz button mushrooms
6 tablespoons olive oil
2 tablespoons tarragon vinegar
1 teaspoon sugar
$\frac{1}{4}$ teaspoon dry mustard
$\frac{1}{2}$ teaspoon salt
freshly ground black pepper
1 tablespoon chopped gherkin
1 tablespoon chopped parsley
1 tablespoon chopped capers

Remove stalks from mushrooms. Wipe mushroom caps
with a clean damp cloth and place in a bowl.
Put olive oil, vinegar, sugar, mustard, salt, pepper
and chopped gherkin, parsley and capers into a screw-top
jar and shake well until ingredients are mixed together.
Pour dressing over mushrooms and allow to stand for 1 hour.
Serve Mushrooms Vinaigrette chilled with slices of French bread,
if desired, to dip into the dressing.

Mushrooms Vinaigrette (left),
Cucumber Hors d'Oeuvre (back),
stuffed olives (front) and
Zucchini Hors d'Oeuvre (right)

Iced Tomato Juice

Serves 4

1 lb fresh or canned tomatoes
2 teaspoons Worcestershire sauce
1 teaspoon sugar
salt and pepper

If using fresh tomatoes select ripe ones. Place
tomatoes in a blender and mix to a purée. Strain
tomato purée and season juice with Worcestershire sauce,
sugar and salt and pepper to taste.
Serve chilled with an ice cube in each glass or
thinned to taste with iced water.
Variation: Add 1 small finely chopped onion to
the tomatoes before mixing in the blender.

Chilled Chicken Soup

Serves 6

2 × 15 oz cans condensed cream of chicken soup
1 cup milk
1 cup water
$\frac{1}{4}$ teaspoon dried tarragon
1 carrot, finely grated

Place all ingredients, except carrot, in a saucepan
and heat gently, stirring until smooth. Cool, then
chill in refrigerator for 3–4 hours.
Serve soup in chilled individual soup bowls and add
a little grated carrot to each portion.

Oyster Cocktail

Serves 4–6

2 dozen oysters
½ cup shredded lettuce
parsley sprigs and wedges of lemon for garnish
brown bread and butter for serving
Sauce:
½ cup cream
2 tablespoons tomato sauce or purée
1 tablespoon Worcestershire sauce
2–3 drops Tabasco sauce
1 tablespoon white vinegar
1 teaspoon anchovy paste
juice of 1 lemon
pinch of dry mustard
pinch of nutmeg
salt
freshly ground pepper

Prepare oysters. Place shredded lettuce in individual
glasses, place oysters on top of lettuce and chill in
refrigerator.
Sauce:
Whip cream lightly and mix in the sauces, vinegar,
anchovy paste, lemon juice, and seasonings. Add salt
and pepper to taste.
Pour the sauce over the prepared oysters. Garnish each
glass with a sprig of parsley and a wedge of lemon. Chill
until ready to serve.
Serve with thin brown bread and butter sandwiches.

21

Pawpaw with Smoked Ham

Serves 6

1 small pawpaw (or melon)
4 oz thinly sliced raw smoked ham
freshly ground black pepper
parsley sprigs for garnish

Cut pawpaw into 6 equal segments, remove seeds. Chill
pawpaw well.
To serve, place pawpaw on 6 individual small plates.
Lay overlapping slices of smoked ham over each piece
of pawpaw and sprinkle with freshly ground black pepper.
Serve immediately, garnished with sprigs of parsley.
Note: Raw smoked ham is obtainable at high quality
delicatessen stores.

Mushroom Liver Pâté

Serves 8–12

4 oz mushrooms, finely chopped
1 oz butter
8 oz cream cheese
8 oz liverwurst
2 tablespoons wine vinegar

Sauté chopped mushrooms in melted butter in a frying pan until golden brown. Drain well, add to remaining ingredients and beat well. Pack mixture into an oiled loaf tin, previously lined with aluminium foil, and chill in refrigerator.
Unmould pâté on to a serving plate and serve with crisp savoury biscuits and accompany with crisp radishes.
Note: Pâté will keep, covered, for several days in a refrigerator.

Tomato
Avocado
Appetizer

Serves 6

6 large tomatoes
2 ripe avocado pears
3 tablespoons lemon juice
salt and pepper
pinch of chilli powder
6 salted almonds or cashew nuts for garnish

Wash tomatoes and dry with a clean tea towel. Cut a
slice from the top of each tomato and scoop out pulp
carefully with a teaspoon. Turn tomatoes upside down
to drain.
Cut avocados in half, remove seed. Scoop out avocado
flesh and mash to a smooth paste with the lemon juice.
Add salt and pepper to taste and mix in chilli powder.
Season inside of tomatoes with salt and pepper and stuff
with avocado mixture. Chill for at least 1 hour.
Serve on individual plates with a salted nut on each
stuffed tomato.

Iced Tomato Yoghurt Soup

Serves 4

2½ cups tomato juice
1¼ cups yoghurt
¼ cup finely chopped celery
1 tablespoon lemon juice
salt and pepper
chopped parsley or chives for garnish

Mix all ingredients together, except parsley, and chill
well.
Serve chilled soup in a bowl sitting in a larger bowl
of ice cubes. Garnish with chopped parsley or chives.

Chilled Tomato Parsley Soup

Serves 4–6

1 lb stewed fresh or canned tomatoes
juice of ½ lemon
1 teaspoon salt
1 slice of onion
parsley sprigs
1 × 15 oz can condensed consommé
2 tablespoons chopped parsley and 1 slice lemon
for garnish

Place tomatoes, lemon juice, salt, onion and a few
parsley sprigs in a blender and mix until smooth and
well blended. Mix tomato purée with consommé. Chill
well. Serve soup chilled garnished with chopped parsley and
thin slices of lemon.

Chilled Coconut Shrimp Soup

Serves 4–6

$\frac{1}{4}$ cup sliced shallots (scallions)
1 clove garlic, crushed
2 teaspoons anchovy paste
1 teaspoon sugar
$\frac{1}{2}$ tablespoon soy sauce
$\frac{1}{2}$ teaspoon salt
$\frac{1}{4}$ teaspoon ground black pepper
2 coriander seeds
$\frac{1}{4}$ teaspoon Tabasco sauce
2 cups coconut milk (see page 53)
$1\frac{1}{4}$ cups cream
1 lb peeled shrimps
1 teaspoon grated lemon rind

Pound to a paste the shallots, garlic, anchovy paste,
sugar, soy sauce, salt, pepper, coriander seeds and
Tabasco sauce. Mix with the coconut milk and cream in
a clean saucepan. Cook over a low heat for 10 minutes.
Add the shrimps and lemon rind and cook for a further
five minutes. Cool and chill well.
Serve chilled soup in chilled soup bowls.
Note: Small prawns may be used if shrimps are not
available.

Chilled Orange Tomato Soup

Serves 4

1 × 10 oz can condensed tomato soup
$1\frac{1}{4}$ cups orange juice
$\frac{1}{2}$ cup cold water
$\frac{1}{4}$ teaspoon dried basil
salt and pepper
$\frac{1}{2}$ cup cream, whipped, or yoghurt

Put tomato soup in a bowl and gradually stir in
orange juice and water. Add basil and chill for at
least 1 hour.
Before serving, season to taste with salt and pepper.
Serve chilled soup in 4 chilled soup bowls and top
each with a tablespoon of lightly whipped cream.

Gazpacho

Serves 6

2 lb tomatoes
½ cucumber
1 green pepper
1 red pepper
6 shallots (scallions)
1 tablespoon olive oil
1 tablespoon wine vinegar
1 cup chilled water
1 clove of garlic, crushed
salt
freshly ground black pepper
the yolk of a hard-boiled egg for garnish
ice cubes

Remove skin from tomatoes and mix to a purée in a
blender, or press through a sieve with a wooden spoon.
Peel the cucumber and dice finely. Cut peppers in half,
remove seeds and dice peppers finely. Slice the shallots
thinly.
Stir the prepared vegetables into the tomato purée with
the olive oil, vinegar and chilled water. Add the crushed
garlic and season to taste with salt and pepper. Chill
well.
Serve the cold soup in chilled soup bowls. Sprinkle
sieved egg yolk in the centre of each portion and add an
ice cube just before serving.

30

Zucchini Hors d'Oeuvre

Serves 4–6

1 lb small zucchini
1 onion
1 teaspoon salt
$\frac{1}{2}$ pint white vinegar
$\frac{1}{2}$ cup sugar
1 teaspoon celery or mustard seeds
$\frac{1}{2}$ teaspoon turmeric
$\frac{1}{2}$ teaspoon dry mustard

Wash zucchini and cut into thin rings. Peel onion and slice thinly. Place zucchini and onion into a bowl, add salt and cover with water. Allow to stand for 1 hour. Drain well.
Place remaining ingredients in a saucepan and bring to the boil. Pour over zucchini and allow to stand for a further 1 hour. Chill.
Serve with tuna or hard-boiled eggs and stuffed olives.

Prawn Cocktail

Serves 6

2–3 cups peeled prawns
1 cup finely chopped celery
lemon wedges and parsley sprigs for garnish
Sauce:
8 tablespoons tomato sauce or purée
6 tablespoons lemon juice
3–4 drops Tabasco sauce
3 teaspoons horseradish sauce
$\frac{1}{2}$ cup cream, optional
salt and pepper

Cut peeled prawns into 1 inch pieces if using large
'king' prawns. Mix prawns with celery and place in
6 individual glasses.
Sauce: Mix all ingredients together. Add cream if
desired. Season to taste with salt and pepper.
Pour sauce over prawns and chill.
Serve cocktail chilled, garnished with lemon wedges
and parsley.

The Main Course

It is most important in the heat of summer, when
appetites are jaded, to make sure that the Main Course
of the meal is deliciously tempting and looks
refreshing.

The recipes I have included in this chapter include
many cool, nourishing fish and meat dishes. Shell fish
such as crab, crayfish and prawns should be as fresh as
possible, carefully prepared and served with flavoursome
dressings. The dressing may be a rich and creamy
mayonnaise or a sharp and tangy French dressing.

A rich, chilled fish or chicken mousse may also be served
for The Main Course. Accompany it with crisp and
crunchy salad vegetables to add interesting texture to
the meal.

The cold meat dishes are a joy to the active housewife
for they may be cooked ahead in the cool of the evening,
when the temperature drops, and chilled ready for serving
in the heat of the next day. Cold joints of meat make
ideal summer party fare.

Tasty cold meat loaf is another family favourite, easy
to make and easy to serve.

Meat has a natural delicious flavour of its own, but
this should be added to in hot climates, by cooking with
hot spices, vegetable flavourings and even wine, cider
or beer. Remember also when serving cold meat that when
food is chilled it sometimes tends to lose some flavour.
If possible, remove cold meat dishes from the refrigerator
$\frac{1}{2}$–1 hour before serving so that they can develop their
natural flavour again at room temperature. It is also
a good idea to serve hot fruit chutneys, pickles, relishes
and mustard with cold meat in hot weather, in order to
add 'pep' to the flavour.

Baked Ham

Barbecues are a popular way to feed family and friends.
A mid-day barbecue or an evening barbecue is always a
happy, relaxing affair. Food may be quite simple, chops,
sausages or steaks, or you may serve a more elaborate dish
such as kebabs.
Try the exciting barbecue recipes in this chapter for
Lamb Sosaties or Beef Sate or Barbecued Spiced Scallops.
These all use spicy marinades which are easy to make in
advance and the food is therefore full of delicious flavour.
Serve with a refreshing salad and potato salad or rice
to complete the meal and make your barbecues a special
summer event.
Hot, spicy dishes, such as curries, are also excellent
hot weather food. Curries, like many cold meat dishes,
may be prepared in the cool of the evening and reheated
and served the next day. This gives the curry time to
mature in flavour. Hot spicy dishes cool the body and
they should be accompanied by hot lime or mango pickles
and chutneys, and refreshing sambals (side dishes) such as sliced
banana sprinkled with lime or lemon juice, or cool
cucumber, sliced thinly and mixed with natural yoghurt.
Take a lesson from other hot climate countries and add
spices to your main course, whether cold meat or a fish
dish or hot, spicy barbecues and curries. Accompany
them with cool and unusual side dishes and salads.
Jaded appetites will be stimulated and hot weather meals
will be a real pleasure.

Baked Ham

Serves 10–12

Time approx 2 hours.
Temperature 400–450°F. reducing to 350–375°F.
½ leg of ham weighing approx. 5 lb
dry mustard
cloves
1 cup cider
4 tablespoons brown sugar
pineapple slices
maraschino cherries for garnish

Ask your butcher to strip the skin off the ham. Rub
dry mustard over the ham and stud the fat side with
cloves.
Place ham on a rack in a roasting pan and bake in a hot
oven for 20 minutes. Reduce temperature to moderate.
Pour cider over ham and bake for a further 1 hour 20 minutes,
basting occasionally. Sprinkle 2 tablespoons brown sugar
over ham and bake for a further 30 minutes without basting.
During the last 15 minutes, place pineapple rings around
ham and sprinkle with remaining brown sugar.
Place baked ham on a carving board and garnish with
glazed pineapple rings and maraschino cherries.
Serve ham cold with French mustard or Horseradish Cream
(see page 61) and Green Salad (see page 84)
Note: If ham is already cooked, reduce baking time to
30 minutes. A can of ham may be glazed and baked in
the same way.

Prawn Salad

Serves 6–8

2–3 lb small prawns in shells
2 tablespoons olive oil
$\frac{1}{4}$ cup sliced shallots (scallions)
2 cloves garlic, crushed
1 cup chopped green pepper
2 tablespoons soy sauce
1 apple, peeled and grated
$\frac{1}{4}$ cup roasted salted peanuts
1 cup coconut milk or yoghurt

Peel prawns and refrigerate until required.
Heat oil in a small frying pan or skillet and fry
the shallots and garlic for 3 minutes. Cool for 5
minutes. Mix with the chopped green pepper, soy sauce,
grated apple, peanuts and coconut milk. Pour over the
prawns and chill for 1 hour.
Serve salad chilled accompanied with Green Bean Salad
(see page 82).

Prawn Salad with Green Bean Salad

Crayfish/ Lobster Mayonnaise

Serves 2

1 × 1½ lb crayfish or lobster
1½ cups mayonnaise (see page 41)
2 tablespoons cream
2–3 drops Tabasco sauce

If the crayfish is alive, boil gently in salted
water for 15 minutes per pound. Cool in the liquid,
drain well and leave until cold.
To prepare crayfish, first remove claws then lay on
a chopping board on the back of the shell. Holding
the head firmly with the left hand, cut the crayfish
down the centre with a heavy chopping knife. Cut down
the centre of the tail and split the crayfish in half
lengthways. Remove the sac in the head and the grey
tube from the centre of the tail.
Remove the meat carefully. Crack claws and remove the
meat with a skewer. Place the claw meat in the head
shell. Slice the tail meat and return to the tail
shell.
Mix mayonnaise with cream and Tabasco sauce. Coat
crayfish meat with mayonnaise and serve remainder in
a sauceboat.
Serve garnished with hearts of lettuce or tomato
segments accompanied with Potato Salad (see page 90)

Mayonnaise

Makes 1½ cups

2 egg yolks
½ teaspoon salt
¼ teaspoon sugar
½ teaspoon dry mustard
pinch of white pepper
1 teaspoon lemon juice
1¼ cups olive oil
2–3 tablespoons white wine vinegar

Place the egg yolks in a mixing bowl, add seasonings
and lemon juice and mix until smooth, using a wooden
spoon or a sauce whisk.
Add 2 tablespoons oil, 2–3 drops at a time, stirring
continuously. Add 1 tablespoon vinegar and mix to the
consistency of cream.
Continue to add oil slowly, whisking continuously.
As the mayonnaise sauce thickens, add the oil more
quickly in a steady stream, whisking continuously. Add
a little vinegar from time to time to prevent
mayonnaise from becoming too thick.
When complete the mayonnaise should be stiff enough
to hold its shape.
Serve with fresh seafood or use to combine ingredients
in salads.

Dressed Crab

Serves 1

1 × 1–2 lb crab
salt and pepper
$\frac{1}{4}$ teaspoon dry mustard
1 hard-boiled egg
crisp lettuce leaves for garnish

If the crab is alive, boil it gently in salted water
for 15 minutes per pound. Cool crab in the liquid, then
take out and leave until quite cold.
To dress crab, first remove big claws and twist off the
small claws. Remove the crab's undershell.
Remove and discard the small sac from the top of the
crab's shell, any green matter and the spongy fingers
or lungs which lie around the big shell.
Scrape the brown creamy part of the crab into a bowl.
Remove the white flesh from the crab, separating it from
the inner shell with a skewer or a pointed vegetable knife.
Wash the shell well, using a small brush if necessary,
dry well.
Crack the big claws, remove all the meat and shred it using
a fork. Mix all the white meat together. Mix the brown
creamy part with salt, pepper and mustard. Place the brown
mixture across the centre of the shell with the white meat
on either side. Garnish with chopped egg white and sieved
egg yolk.
Serve dressed crab on a bed of lettuce leaves and accompany
with segments of lemon or mayonnaise.

Herring Salad

Serves 6

3 pickled herrings or rollmops
1 cup diced cooked beetroot
2 cups diced cooked potato
1 onion, finely chopped
1 apple, peeled and chopped
1 dill pickled cucumber, chopped
1 cup sour cream or mayonnaise (see page 41)
salt and pepper
lettuce and 2 hard-boiled eggs for garnish

Cut the herrings into bite-sized pieces. Mix herring
with prepared beetroot, potato, onion, apple and pickled
cucumber. Fold in mayonnaise until ingredients are well
coated. Season to taste with salt and pepper. Chill.
Serve Herring Salad on a bed of lettuce leaves and garnish
with segments of hard-boiled egg.

Salami Salad

Serves 6

8 oz salami
4 oz gruyère or emmenthal cheese
½ cup diced celery
2 cups diced cooked potato
6 shallots, sliced (scallions)
1 cup mayonnaise or yoghurt (for mayonnaise see page 41)
salt and pepper

Peel salami and slice thinly. Cut cheese into
thin strips. Mix salami and cheese with celery,
potato, shallots and mayonnaise. Season to taste
with salt and pepper.
Serve Salami Salad with Green Salad (see page 84).

Seafood Salad

Serves 6–8

1 lettuce
8 oz prawns
8 oz crab
8 oz crayfish or lobster
8 oz white fish
4 tomatoes
8 olives
Dressing:
1½ cups mayonnaise (see page 41)
juice of 1 lemon
1 tablespoon finely chopped onion
½ teaspoon dry mustard
pinch of saffron
salt and pepper

Line a salad bowl with crisp lettuce leaves. Prepare
prawns, crab and crayfish and steam white fish. Cut into
1 inch cubes and place attractively on top of lettuce.
Garnish with tomato wedges and olives.
Chill and serve with dressing.
Dressing: Mix mayonnaise with lemon juice, onion and
mustard. Dissolve saffron in a little hot water and stir
into the dressing. Add salt and pepper to taste. Chill
before serving.
Note: To steam fish, place skin side down on a plate
over a pan of gently boiling water. Season with pepper
and salt, add a little milk, cover with saucepan lid
and steam for 10–15 minutes or until fish is cooked.

Soused Fish

Serves 6

Time 3 hours
Temperature 300–325° F.

6 herring or mullet
1 onion, sliced
vinegar
water
4 bay leaves
2 cloves
12 allspice
2 blades of mace
1 teaspoon salt

Clean herrings and remove backbone. Lay herrings,
skin side down on working surface and place sliced
onion on centre of each fish. Roll fish up from
head to tail, secure with a toothpick.
Place fish in an ovenproof dish and add vinegar and
water to cover in the proportion of 3 parts vinegar to
1 part water. Add herbs, spices and salt.
Cover and cook in a slow oven for 3 hours, or until
fish is cooked. The liquid must not boil.
Transfer fish to a serving dish, strain liquor over,
cool then chill in refrigerator. The liquor sets in a
soft jelly.
Serve Soused Fish with Cucumber Salad (see page 86).

Soused Fish with Cucumber Salad

Salmon Mousse

Serves 8–10

6 hard-boiled eggs
4 gherkins
1½ tablespoons gelatine
1 cup hot water
1 cup white wine
½ white vinegar
½ cup lemon juice
1 × 15 oz can salmon
salt and pepper
lettuce leaves and tomatoes for garnish

Rinse a mould with cold water and decorate with
slices of hard-boiled egg and gherkin. Dissolve
gelatine in hot water, and stir in wine, vinegar
and lemon juice. Pour a little gelatine mixture
over egg and gherkin decoration and refrigerate until set.
Drain salmon and flake well with a fork. Chop any
remaining hard-boiled egg and gherkin and mix with
the salmon. Add gelatine mixture and season to taste
with salt and pepper. Pour mixture into prepared
mould and refrigerate until set.
Turn out on to a flat serving plate and garnish with
small lettuce leaves and tomato wedges. Serve chilled
with Cucumber Sauce (see page 49).

Cucumber
Sauce

Makes approx. 3–4 cups

2 small cucumbers
sugar
1¼ cups cream
4 tablespoons wine vinegar
salt
cayenne pepper

Peel cucumbers, remove seeds, and chop flesh into
fine dice. Sprinkle with sugar and leave to stand
for 1½–2 hours.
Whip cream until stiff, add well-drained cucumber,
vinegar and salt and cayenne pepper to taste. Mix
gently until ingredients are evenly combined.
Serve Cucumber Sauce immediately with Salmon Mousse
(see page 48) or a fish salad.
Note: The sauce will become thin if left to stand
before serving.

Cold Baked Silverside of Beef

Serves 10–12

Time 3–4 hours
Temperature 325–350°F.

5–6 lb silverside of beef or top sirloin roast (salted)
2 carrots
2 onions
1 clove garlic, crushed
1 bay leaf
6 peppercorns
2 cloves
1 cup beer or red wine

Soak the beef in cold water for at least 2 hours before baking it.
Place the beef in a large ovenproof casserole or pot-roaster. Peel the carrots and onions, cut into chunky pieces and add to the casserole. Add the crushed garlic, bay leaf, peppercorns, cloves, beer or wine and sufficient cold water to cover the beef.
Cover and cook in a moderately slow oven for 3–4 hours or until tender. Test with a skewer or a fork, it should come out easily if the meat is cooked.
Remove the beef and place in a large bowl. Put a plate or a board on top and a heavy weight. Leave to stand overnight if possible.
Serve beef cold with a fruit chutney, Tomato Salad (see page 90 and Green Salad (see page 84)
Note: The stock may be used to make a delicious chilled soup.

Cold Baked Silverside
of Beef with Green Salad

Jellied Chicken

Serves 8–10

1 × 2½–3 lb chicken
1 onion
1 stalk celery
1 bay leaf
1 sprig parsley
salt
4 oz sliced ham
1 hard-boiled egg
1 gherkin
1 tablespoon gelatine
1 cup hot water
1 cup canned consommé
watercress sprigs for garnish

Wipe chicken with a clean, damp cloth. Peel onion
and cut celery into small pieces. Place onion, celery,
bay leaf and parsley into chicken's breast cavity. Sprinkle
chicken with salt, wrap securely in greased greaseproof
paper and steam for 1 hour or until tender. Cool.
Cut ham into neat circles, cut egg into circles and slice
gherkin into leaf shapes. Rinse a mould and decorate with
ham, egg and gherkin. Dissolve gelatine in hot water,
and mix with consommé. Pour a little jelly over decoration
and refrigerate until set. Remove flesh from chicken and
cut into ½ inch pieces. Chop scraps of remaining ham
finely. Mix chicken and ham with remaining gelatine
mixture, place gently over decoration in mould and chill
until set.
Unmould Jellied Chicken on to a serving plate, garnish
with watercress and serve with mixed salads or Cole Slaw
(see page 78).

No. *10*

Coconut Milk

Coconut milk may be made from fresh coconuts or desiccated coconut. Frozen coconut milk is also obtainable from leading delicatessens and grocery departments.

Fresh Coconut Milk

1 cup grated fresh coconut
2 cups hot water

Prepare coconut and place in a bowl. Add hot water and allow to stand for 30 minutes. Strain well through a fine sieve or through a piece of muslin.

Desiccated Coconut Milk

1 cup desiccated coconut
2 cups hot milk

Place desiccated coconut in a bowl and add hot milk. Allow to stand for 30 minutes. Strain well through a fine sieve or through a piece of muslin.
Note: Yoghurt may be used in place of coconut milk in the recipes given in this book.

Cold Loin of Pork Oriental

Serves 8–10

Time 2½–3 hours
Temperature 350–400°F.

1 × 5 lb loin of pork
dry mustard
½ cup sherry
½ cup soy sauce
1 tablespoon grated fresh ginger or 2 teaspoons ground ginger
2–4 cloves garlic, crushed
8 oz red currant jelly
extra 2 tablespoons sherry
extra 2 tablespoons soy sauce

Ask your butcher to bone and roll the loin of pork. Rub
pork with mustard.
Prepare a marinade by mixing together the sherry, soy sauce,
ginger and garlic. Pour marinade over pork and marinate for
2 hours, turning meat occasionally.
Place pork on a rack in a roasting pan and cook in a
moderate oven for 2½–3 hours or until meat is cooked.
Baste pork with marinade while roasting.
Place red currant jelly in a saucepan and melt over a
low heat. Stir in extra sherry and soy sauce and heat
for 1 minute. Spoon jelly over loin of pork and stand
in a cold place.
Serve cold roast pork at room temperature, if possible,
accompanied with Green Salad (see page 84), Cabbage
Salad (see page 81) and Potato Salad (see page 90).

Glazed Baked Bacon

Serves 10–12

Time 2 hours
Temperature 375–400°F.

1 joint of bacon weighing 4–4½ lb
cloves
1 onion
1 carrot
2 stalks celery
2½ cups cider or beer
2 tablespoons brown sugar
1 × 15 oz can apricot halves
10–12 maraschino or glacé cherries
sprigs of parsley or watercress for garnish

Soak the bacon in cold water for 6 hours if smoked,
for 2 hours if unsmoked. Drain well and remove the
rind. Place bacon on a rack in a roasting pan and
stud the fat side with cloves. Cut vegetables into
chunky pieces and add to bacon in roasting pan. Pour
cider over and sprinkle sugar over bacon joint.
Cover roasting pan with aluminium foil and cook in a
moderately hot oven for 1½ hours. Remove foil and place
drained apricot halves and cherries attractively on top
of bacon, securing with toothpicks. Baste well and cook,
uncovered for a further 20–30 minutes, basting occasionally.
Place bacon on a carving board. Allow to cool.
Garnish bacon with sprigs of parsley or watercress and
serve cold with a fruit chutney, Potato Salad (see page 90) and
Green Salad (see page 84).

56

Peach Chutney

Makes 3 pints

16 medium size peaches (to fill 8 cups)
1 cup raisins
1½ cups brown sugar, firmly packed
¾ cup cider vinegar
1 teaspoon cinnamon
½ teaspoon ground cloves
2 teaspoons mustard seed
½ cup chopped nuts, optional

Peel peaches, remove stones and slice the fruit. Measure
8 cups of fruit and place in a large heavy-based pan. Add
remaining ingredients, except nuts. Bring to the boil and
simmer, uncovered, stirring frequently, for 45 minutes
or until mixture has thickened. Add nuts, if desired, and
cook a further 2 minutes.
Pour chutney into 6 sterilized ½ pint jars to within ½ inch
of the top and seal. Store in refrigerator and use within
2–3 weeks.
Serve chutney with slices of cold meat and salad.
Variation: Try making this chutney with apricots,
nectarines or mangoes.

Cold Fillet of Beef

Serves 8–10

Time 45 minutes
Temperature 400–450°F.

1 × 3 lb fillet of beef
freshly ground black pepper
2 oz butter
2 tablespoons olive oil

Trim fillet of beef, removing all fat and tissue. Sprinkle
with freshly ground black pepper. Melt butter, mix with
olive oil and brush all over the beef. Wrap fillet of beef
in greased aluminium foil. Place on a rack in a roasting
pan and cook in a hot oven for 30 minutes. Unwrap foil
and allow beef to cook for a further 15 minutes or until
cooked as desired.
Transfer beef to a carving board and leave to cool.
Serve beef cold, carved in thin slices, and accompanied
with French mustard or Horseradish Cream (see page 61) and
mixed salads.

Cold Fillet of Beef
with Potato Salad and Tomato Salad

Cold Roast Lamb with Coriander

Serves 6–8

Time 1½ hours
Temperature 350–375°F.

1 × 3 lb leg of lamb
3–4 cloves of garlic
1 tablespoon coriander seeds
salt and pepper
2 tablespoons butter or vegetable oil

Make a few deep cuts in the leg of lamb with a
sharp pointed vegetable or filleting knife. Peel
the garlic and cut each clove into thin slices. Crush
the coriander seeds. Place the sliced garlic and coriander
seeds into the incisions in the lamb.
Sprinkle the leg of lamb with salt and pepper and rub into
the flesh using clean hands.
Place the meat on a rack in a roasting pan, add butter
or oil and cook in a moderate oven for 1½ hours or until
cooked. Remove from roasting pan, place on a carving board
and allow to cool.
Serve cold, carved in thick slices and accompany with
red currant jelly, Green Bean Salad (see page 82) or Pea
Salad (see page 81).

Horseradish Cream
Makes $1\frac{1}{2}$–2 cups

$1\frac{1}{2}$ cups fresh or sour cream
1 × 5 oz jar horseradish relish

If using fresh cream, whip until stiff and mix
with the horseradish relish.
If using sour cream, mix the two ingredients
together until evenly combined.
Chill Horseradish Cream before serving.
Delicious served with cold roast beef and cold
baked ham.

Cold Veal with Lemon
Serves 6–8

1 × 3 lb loin or leg of veal
salt and pepper
2 teaspoons nutmeg
$\frac{1}{2}$ cup water or chicken stock
3 lemons

Rub veal with salt, pepper and nutmeg and place in a
large, heavy-based pan. Add water, cover and simmer
very gently for 30 minutes. Add rind and juice of
lemons and continue to simmer, covered, for $1\frac{1}{2}$–2 hours
or until veal is cooked.
Remove veal from pan, place on a serving plate, pour
juices over and leave to cool.
Serve veal cold, carved in thick slices, and accompanied
with Citrus Green Salad (see page   ).

Barbecued Beef Sate

Serves 6

2 lb rump steak
2 tablespoons soy sauce
1 tablespoon honey
2 cloves garlic, crushed
1 teaspoon ground coriander
1 teaspoon caraway seeds
$\frac{1}{4}$ teaspoon chilli powder
2 tablespoons vegetable oil

Cut steak into 1 inch cubes and place in a large bowl.
Mix remaining ingredients together and pour over
meat. Marinate for 1 hour, stirring occasionally.
Thread meat on to six skewers. Barbecue over hot
coals, turning occasionally, for 10 minutes or until
cooked to desired taste. Baste with marinade during
cooking.
Serve Beef Sate with Barbecue Sauce (see page 64) and
Green Salad (see page 84).

Barbecue Sauce

Makes 2 cups

½ cup finely chopped onion
2 tablespoons brown sugar
2 tablespoons lime juice
1 tablespoon soy sauce
½ cup tomato sauce
½ cup water
freshly ground black pepper

Place all ingredients except pepper in a saucepan and heat gently, stirring continuously, until sugar is dissolved. Add pepper to taste.
Serve Barbecue Sauce with barbecued meat. Particularly delicious with Barbecued Beef Sate (see page   ).
Note: Lemon juice may be used in place of fresh lime juice.

Raisin Yellow Rice

Serves 6

½ oz butter
3 cups chicken stock or 3 cups water and
   3 chicken stock cubes
1½ cups long grain rice
2 tablespoons sugar
1 teaspoon turmeric
½ cup seedless raisins
salt and pepper

Melt butter in a saucepan, add chicken stock and bring to the boil. Add rice and stir well. Turn down heat. Add remaining ingredients, with salt and pepper to taste and simmer, covered, for 20 minutes, or until liquid has been absorbed and grains are tender.
Serve hot with barbecued meat.

Barbecued Spiced Scallops

Serves 6

2 lb scallops
1 clove garlic, crushed
1 teaspoon grated root ginger
1 tablespoon sugar
½ cup soy sauce
½ cup dry sherry or sake
1 green pepper
4 oz small mushrooms

Place scallops in a bowl and add the next 5 ingredients.
Leave to marinate for 2 hours, at room temperature, stirring
occasionally.
Cut pepper in half, remove seeds and cut pepper into 1 inch
pieces. Wipe mushrooms with a clean, damp cloth.
Drain scallops and thread on to six skewers, alternating
with green pepper and mushrooms.
Barbecue over hot coals, turning occasionally, for 10–15
minutes or until cooked to taste. Baste with the marinade
before and during cooking.
Serve barbecued scallops hot with Spinach Salad (see page 92)
or Cucumber Salad (see page 86).

Beef Curry

Serves 4

1 lb beef topside steak
1 tablespoon ground coriander
1 teaspoon ground turmeric
$\frac{1}{2}$ teaspoon cumin
$\frac{1}{4}$ teaspoon chilli powder
pinch of ground cinnamon
2 cloves
1 bay leaf
3 tablespoons vinegar
2 tablespoons vegetable oil
1 onion, chopped
1 clove garlic, crushed
1 teaspoon salt
$\frac{3}{4}$ cup water and 1 beef stock cube

Cut beef into 1 inch cubes.
Mix and pound the spices with the vinegar to form a paste.
Heat oil in a heavy saucepan and fry onion and garlic
gently for 5 minutes. Add curry paste and fry for
2–3 minutes, stirring continuously. Add beef and cook
gently, stirring occasionally, until beef changes
colour. Add salt, water and beef stock cube, cover and
simmer for 1 hour.
Taste curry before serving and adjust flavour if
necessary.
Serve curry with boiled rice and sambals or side dishes such
as lime chutney, mango pickle, sliced banana, tomatoes in
lemon juice, sliced cucumber in yoghurt.

Beef Curry with side dishes

Spiced Chicken and Pineapple

Serves 4–6

1 × 3 lb chicken
$\frac{3}{4}$ teaspoon chilli powder
1 teaspoon salt
3 cloves garlic, crushed
$\frac{1}{2}$ cup sliced shallots (scallions)
1 teaspoon anchovy paste
3 tablespoons vegetable oil
$1\frac{1}{2}$ cups diced fresh or canned pineapple
2 teaspoons grated lime or lemon rind
2 tablespoons lime or lemon juice
1 cup coconut cream (see page 69)
2 teaspoons soy sauce
$\frac{1}{2}$ cup sautéed sliced shallots (scallions) for garnish

Cut the chicken from the bones and cut into 1 inch cubes.
Mix together chilli powder, salt, crushed garlic, shallots and anchovy paste. Add chicken, mix well and leave to stand for 1 hour.
Heat oil in a heavy-based saucepan and fry the chicken and pineapple until chicken is lightly browned. Add rind, lime juice, coconut cream and soy sauce. Cover and simmer over a low heat for 30 minutes or until tender.
Serve hot, sprinkled with sautéed sliced shallots for garnish, and accompany with boiled rice and hot spicy chutney.
Note: Good quality anchovy paste is obtainable from leading delicatessens.

Coconut Cream

Coconut cream may be made from fresh coconuts or desiccated coconut. Frozen coconut cream is obtainable from leading delicatessens and grocery departments.

Fresh Coconut Cream

2 cups grated fresh coconut
1 cup hot water

Prepare coconut and place in a bowl. Add hot water and allow to stand for 30 minutes. Strain well through a fine sieve or through a piece of muslin.

Desiccated Coconut Cream

1 cup desiccated coconut
1 cup cream

Place desiccated coconut in a bowl. Heat cream gently until almost boiling and pour over coconut. Allow to stand for 30 minutes. Strain well through a fine sieve or through a piece of muslin.
Note: Fresh cream may be used in place of coconut cream in the recipes given in this book.

Salads

When summer comes we always think of salads and
slimming! Salads should be imaginative, crisp,
refreshing and delicious.

There are always interesting, colourful salad
vegetables in season to make tasty, attractive
salads. Add variety of flavour and texture to these
with the addition of fruit, nuts or fresh herbs.

Citrus fruit is particularly refreshing in mixed
salads as it contains a lot of juice. Use segments
of grapefruit, slices of orange or lemon or lime juice
in your salads. Pineapple is another refreshing salad
ingredient.

Meat, fish or eggs may be added to mixed salads to make
a substantial, balanced meal. Toss salads in cool
dressings made from mayonnaise, sour cream, yoghurt
or an acidic French dressing.

Salad plants must always be fresh and crisp and require
careful preparation. Ideally, salad greens should be
used straight from the garden, but if this is not
possible, they should be washed and dried carefully
and then crisped up in the refrigerator before serving.

Simple green salads should be tossed in dressing at
the last minute, just before serving, otherwise they
will lose their crispness. This kind of salad, tossed
in French dressing, makes an excellent accompaniment
in hot weather for barbecued fish or meat or quickly
grilled meat.

Two salad 'standbys' are the traditional French
dressing and mayonnaise dressing. French dressing
is made from three parts of olive oil to one part of
vinegar. The vinegar should be a good quality wine
vinegar or herb-flavoured vinegar. Add salt and
freshly-ground pepper to taste. A good pinch of sugar
and dry mustard add flavour. A clove of crushed garlic

Salad vegetables

is another traditional flavouring. Various herbs may
be chopped and added to the dressing to enhance its
flavour; parsley, chives, mint, dill and tarragon
are among the most popular used.
Mayonnaise, another classical dressing, is popular
mixed with salads. It is often served separately in
a sauceboat. However, for refreshingly different
salad dressings in a hot climate, try natural yoghurt,
sour cream, lime juice or lemon juice.
The attraction of a salad depends greatly on its
appearance. It should look light and delicate and
be fresh and neat in presentation. Be adventurous
with your salad creations. Try Serving Red Cole Slaw
with cold pork, Cucumber Salad with cold fish mousse,
Carrot Salad with barbecued meat.
Remember always to prepare the salad ingredients
carefully, taste the dressing and adjust the flavour,
and serve the salad crisp and chilled.

Carrot Salad

Serves 6–8

1 cup soft breadcrumbs
1 oz butter
$\frac{1}{2}$ cup peanuts, shelled
2 cups grated carrot
2 tablespoons vegetable oil
1 tablespoon white vinegar
salt and pepper

Fry breadcrumbs in the butter until crisp and
golden. Add peanuts and mix well. Cool. Add grated
carrot, oil, vinegar and salt and pepper to taste. Toss
lightly.
Chill before serving.

Avocado Fancy Salad Bowl

Serves 6–8

1 lettuce
1 × 16 oz can asparagus spears
1 × 14 oz can artichoke hearts
1 avocado pear
1 tablespoon pitted, sliced olives
1 quantity French dressing (see page 85)

Wash lettuce, dry well in a clean tea towel, refrigerate
in an air-tight container to crispen.
Drain asparagus and artichokes. Peel avocado pear, remove
seed and cut avocado into slices.
Tear lettuce in bite-sized pieces into a chilled salad
bowl. Add asparagus, artichokes and olives. Add French
dressing and toss gently until all lettuce leaves glisten
with dressing. Arrange avocado slices attractively on
top of salad.
Serve salad immediately. Delicious with Cold Roast
Fillet of Beef (see page 58).

Citrus Green Salad

Serves 6–8

1 lettuce
1 bunch watercress
2 grapefruit
2 oranges
1 quantity French dressing (see page 85)

Prepare lettuce (see Green Salad, page 84) and crispen
in refrigerator.
Wash watercress sprigs and dry in a clean tea towel.
Crispen in refrigerator.
Remove peel carefully from grapefruit and oranges, using
a sharp, serrated knife. Make sure all pith is removed.
Cut grapefruit and oranges into sections and place in
a chilled salad bowl.
Add lettuce, torn into bite-sized pieces, and watercress
sprigs. Pour French dressing over and toss salad gently
with clean hands until each leaf is coated with dressing.
Serve salad immediately. Delicious served with rye bread
and cheese for a quick summer lunch.

Caesar's Salad

Serves 6–8

4 × ¼ inch slices of bread
4 tablespoons olive oil
1 clove garlic, crushed
1 egg
1 lettuce (preferably romaine)
1 × 2 oz can anchovy fillets
1 quantity French dressing (see page 85)
juice of 1 lemon
2 tablespoons Parmesan cheese

Remove crusts from bread and cut each slice into
¼ inch cubes. Heat oil with crushed garlic in a frying
pan and fry croutons until crisp and golden. Drain well
on kitchen paper.
Place the egg in a heatproof bowl, cover with boiling
water and stand for 3 minutes to 'coddle'.
Tear crisp lettuce into bite-sized pieces and place in
a chilled salad bowl. Add drained, chopped anchovy
fillets.
Mix French dressing with lemon juice, pour
over salad and toss gently. Break the coddled egg into
the salad, add Parmesan cheese and toss once again.
Serve salad immediately. This salad blends well with
fish salads.

Beetroot Salad

Serves 8–10

1 tablespoon gelatine
3 tablespoons hot water
2 cups boiling water
3 tablespoons wine vinegar
3 cups chopped cooked beetroot
1 stalk celery, chopped, optional
1 teaspoon horseradish relish
salt and pepper

Dissolve gelatine in 3 tablespoons hot water. Add
boiling water and vinegar. Allow to cool.
Stir in chopped beetroot, celery if desired and horseradish
relish. Season to taste with salt and pepper.
Pour mixture into a previously rinsed mould or a serving
dish and chill in refrigerator until set.
Serve Beetroot Salad with cold beef or ham.

Cole Slaw

Serves 12

1 small firm cabbage
3 red apples
1 cup raisins
Dressing:
6 tablespoons olive oil
1 tablespoon lemon juice
1 tablespoon orange juice
1 tablespoon Worcestershire sauce
2 tablespoons finely chopped onion
1 tablespoon chopped stuffed olives
1 tablespoon chopped parsley
$\frac{1}{2}$ teaspoon dry mustard
$\frac{1}{2}$ teaspoon salt
$\frac{1}{4}$ teaspoon pepper

Shred cabbage finely, removing any coarse stem.
Remove cores from apples, do not peel. Dice apples
and add to cabbage. Add raisins, which have been
previously soaked in $\frac{1}{2}$ cup hot water for 5–10
minutes. Add dressing and toss until salad is evenly
coated.
Serve chilled with cold ham or cold pork.
Dressing: Mix all ingredients together.

Cole Slaw ingredients

Cool Radish Salad

Serves 6–8

1 bunch radishes
1 small cucumber
1¼ cups sour cream
juice of 1 lemon
salt and pepper
extra radishes and parsley sprigs for garnish

Slice radishes into fine circles. Peel cucumber and
slice finely. Mix radishes and cucumber with sour
cream, lemon juice and salt and pepper to taste. Place
in a salad bowl and chill for at least 1 hour.
Garnish salad with extra radishes and parsley and serve
chilled with cold beef or cold meat loaf.

Mushroom Bean Salad

Serves 4–6

1 × 10 oz can lima or broad beans
6 oz mushrooms, sliced
1 teaspoon finely chopped onion
½ teaspoon ground nutmeg
1 quantity French dressing (see page 85)

Drain beans into a strainer and rinse under cold
running water. Drain well.
Mix beans with sliced raw mushrooms, onion and nutmeg.
Pour French dressing over and chill for at least 1 hour.
Serve salad with cold meat or barbecued meat.

Pea Salad

Serves 4–6

1 × 12 oz packet frozen peas
4 oz mushrooms, thinly sliced
2 stalks celery, finely sliced
2 tablespoons sultanas, optional
2 tablespoons olive oil
2 tablespoons wine vinegar
salt and pepper
¼ teaspoon dry mustard
1 teaspoon sugar
1 clove garlic, crushed

Cook the peas according to the directions on the packet.
Drain and cool.
Mix the cold peas with the sliced raw mushrooms and celery
in a salad bowl. Add sultanas if desired.
Place remaining ingredients in a screw-top jar, cover
and shake well. Pour dressing over pea mixture and chill well.

Cabbage Salad

Serves 6–8

the heart of 1 small red cabbage or ½ red cabbage
salt
3 tablespoons olive oil
2 tablespoons white wine vinegar
1 teaspoon sugar
freshly ground pepper
1 onion, finely chopped
2 red eating apples, cored and sliced or diced

Shred cabbage finely, sprinkle with salt and allow
to stand for 1 hour. Press cabbage well to drain
off liquor.
Make dressing by mixing together olive oil, vinegar,
sugar, salt and pepper in a screw-top jar.
Pour dressing over cabbage. Add onion and apple.

Greek Salata

Serves 10–12

3 cups shredded cabbage
1 cup cooked beetroot cut in julienne strips
1 cup cooked green beans
1 tablespoon capers
1 tablespoon chopped olives
1 quantity French dressing (see page 85)

Place prepared cabbage, beetroot and beans in a salad
bowl. Sprinkle capers and olives over salad.
Pour dressing over salad and chill for at least 30
minutes.
Serve salad chilled with cold meat or barbecued meat.

Green Bean Salad

Serves 6–8

$1\frac{1}{2}$ lb green beans
2 large tomatoes, peeled and chopped
1 onion, sliced
1 teaspoon sugar
$\frac{1}{2}$ teaspoon dried oregano
$\frac{1}{2}$ teaspoon salt
freshly ground black pepper
$\frac{1}{4}$ cup olive oil

Top and tail and string beans. Place in a pan of
boiling, salted water and boil for 5 minutes. Drain,
cool and chill.
Gently mix beans with remaining ingredients and chill.
Serve with cold meat or fish salads.

82   Greek Salata

Green Salad

Serves 6–8

1 lettuce
½ cucumber
1 green pepper
½ cup parsley sprigs, optional
1 cup watercress sprigs, optional
1 quantity French dressing (see page 85)

Prepare lettuce. Firstly remove outside leaves which
are dirty, bruised or limp. Remove core of lettuce with
a sharp vegetable knife. Hold lettuce upside down under
a cold flowing tap, allowing water to run into centre
of lettuce. Turn lettuce over and allow to drain. Gently
peel lettuce leaves apart, place in a clean tea towel,
roll up gently and shake well to remove water. Place
lettuce in a plastic container in refrigerator and chill
until crisp.
Peel cucumber and cut into thin slices.
Wash and seed green pepper and cut into thin rings.
Place crisp lettuce, torn into bite-sized pieces, into
a chilled salad bowl. Add prepared cucumber, green pepper
and parsley and watercress sprigs if desired. Pour
French dressing over and gently roll the salad in this
with clean hands until each leaf is glistening with
dressing.
Serve immediately with cold meat or barbecued meat.

French Dressing

3 tablespoons olive oil
1 tablespoon herb flavoured or wine vinegar
1 teaspoon sugar
$\frac{1}{2}$ teaspoon dry mustard
$\frac{1}{2}$ teaspoon salt
freshly ground black pepper
1 clove garlice, crushed
1 tablespoon chopped fresh herbs, optional

Place all ingredients in a screw-top jar and shake
well until evenly mixed.
Alternatively all the dry ingredients may be placed
in a salad bowl and the liquid ingredients added
slowly, whisking continuously until smoothly combined.
Use to dress salads and to dress hors d'oeuvres dishes.
Note: Larger quantities of French Dressing may be
prepared and stored in a screw-top jar in the refrigerator
for a few weeks.
A good quality salad oil may be used instead of olive
oil and white vinegar may be used instead of herb flavoured
or wine vinegar. However, for a good flavoured dressing,
try the given recipe.

Cucumber Salad

Serves 6

2 medium size cucumbers
1 teaspoon salt
1 small onion, finely chopped
3 tablespoons white vinegar
1 tablespoon water
1 teaspoon sugar
$\frac{1}{4}$ teaspoon white pepper

Wash and dry cucumbers and score the skin lengthways
with the prongs of a fork. Slice cucumbers very thinly.
Sprinkle with salt and leave to stand for 1 hour.
Drain off liquid, pressing cucumbers to drain as much
as possible.
Mix remaining ingredients together with salt and pepper
to taste and pour over cucumbers. Chill. Drain off
liquor just before serving.
Serve with cold fish or meat, barbecued meat and
curries.

Barbecued Lamb Sosaties with
Cucumber Salad and Carrot Salad

Waldorf Salad

Serves 4–6

6 red apples
juice of 2 lemons
6 stalks celery, sliced
$\frac{1}{2}$ cup walnut halves
1 cup mayonnaise, sour cream or yoghurt (for mayonnaise see page 41)
1 small lettuce for serving

Remove core from apples. Do not peel. Cut apples
into $\frac{1}{2}$ inch dice and sprinkle with lemon juice. Add
sliced celery and walnuts. Add mayonnaise and toss
gently until well mixed. Chill.
Serve salad chilled in a salad bowl lined with crisp
lettuce leaves. Particularly good served with cold beef or ham.

Rice Salad

Serves 6

2 cups cooked rice
1 onion, finely chopped
$\frac{1}{2}$ cup chopped parsley
$\frac{1}{2}$ cup finely chopped red or green pepper
$\frac{1}{2}$ cup cooked peas, optional
2 quantities French dressing (see page 85)

Mix all the ingredients, except rice, together with
French dressing. Chill for 1 hour at least.
When ready to serve, add cold rice and toss well.
Serve with barbecued meat or fish or with cold meat
or fish salads.

Green
Lychee
Salad

Serves 6–8

1 lettuce
1 bunch watercress
1 × 15 oz can lychees
2 quantities French dressing, made with
    tarragon flavoured wine vinegar or red wine vinegar

Prepare lettuce, wash and dry well. Crispen in an
air-tight container in refrigerator.
Cut sprigs from bunch of watercress just before required.
Wash and dry well. Tear lettuce in bite-sized pieces into
a chilled salad bowl. Add watercress, drained lychees
and French dressing, and toss gently until all the leaves
glisten with dressing.
Serve salad immediately.
Note: Keep watercress fresh by standing the bunch in a
large jug of cold water and place in refrigerator.

Tomato Salad

Serves 4–6

1 lb tomatoes
1 tablespoon chopped fresh basil
   or 1 teaspoon dried basil
finely grated rind of 1 lemon
1 quantity French dressing (see page 85)

Slice tomatoes thinly and place in a flat shallow
dish. Sprinkle tomatoes with basil, lemon rind and
French dressing. Chill for 30 minutes.
Serve Tomato Salad with cold meat, cold fish salads
or barbecued meat.
Variation: Add 2 oranges, peeled and segmented neatly,
for a refreshing salad.

Potato Salad

Serves 4–6

1 lb potatoes
1 small onion, finely chopped
1 Granny Smith apple, peeled and chopped
1 dill pickle, chopped
$1\frac{1}{4}$ cups sour cream
juice of 1 lemon
salt and pepper

Boil potatoes in skins. Drain and cool. Peel
potatoes thinly and cut into $\frac{1}{2}$–1 inch cubes. Add
chopped onion, apple and dill pickle. Add sour cream
and lemon juice and mix gently until potatoes are well
coated. Season to taste with salt and pepper.
Serve chilled in a chilled salad bowl.
Note: Any sweet, crisp apple can be used. The
Granny Smith has a green skin.

          Tomato Salad with orange segments

Spinach Salad

Serves 6

1 lb spinach
$\frac{1}{4}$ lb raw young mushrooms
6 shallots (scallions), sliced
2 tablespoons sesame seeds
2 tablespoons soy sauce
1 tablespoon sugar
3 tablespoons cider vinegar
freshly ground black pepper
1 small onion, thinly sliced
$\frac{1}{4}$ cup crumbled grilled bacon (optional)

Wash spinach carefully, dry in a clean towel. Remove
core from leaves and place spinach in an air-tight
container in refrigerator to crispen.
Slice mushrooms thinly.
Pound sesame seeds in a mortar, or in a heavy bowl using
a wooden spoon. Add soy sauce, sugar and vinegar and mix
well. Add freshly ground black pepper to taste.
Tear crisp spinach into bite-sized pieces and place in
a chilled salad bowl. Add sliced onion, separated into
rings, sliced raw mushrooms and sliced shallots. Add
sesame mixture and toss gently with clean hands, until
every piece of spinach glistens with the dressing.
The salad may be topped with crumbled bacon.
Serve chilled with barbecued meat or with Barbecued
Spiced Scallops (see page 65).

Salade Nicoise

Serves 6

1 × 7 oz can tuna fish
1 × 12 oz packet frozen green beans
4 medium size tomatoes
1 tablespoon chopped parsley, basil or chives
1 small cucumber, sliced
1 quantity French dressing (see page 85)
1 × 2 oz can anchovy fillets
6–12 black olives

Drain fish and flake into a salad bowl.
Cook beans according to directions on packet, drain
well and cool. Place on top of tuna.
Peel tomatoes, cut into segments and add to salad
bowl. Cover with a layer of sliced cucumber. Pour
French dressing over.
Place anchovy fillets on top of salad in lattice
fashion and place an olive in each square. Chill.
Serve salad chilled, accompanied with French bread
and butter and a bottle of chilled white wine.

93

The Dessert Course

Fresh fruit desserts are ideal for hot climates.
They are refreshing and full of delicious, natural
juicy flavours.
Cold sweets using fresh fruit are simple to make and
there are many to choose from. Try the recipes given
in this chapter. Most of them require no cooking at
all so you can keep your kitchen cool. Others require
slight cooking to thicken custards and dissolve gelatine
for soufflés and mousses. All the desserts should be
chilled in the refrigerator before serving.
The most popular hot weather desserts are ice cream,
fruit salad, fruit creams, fruit mousses, soufflés
and jellies.
Fresh fruits form the basis of many of these recipes,
but if they are not available, canned, bottled, frozen
and even dried fruit may be used as an alternative.
Cream may be substituted with evaporated milk. This
has a more definite flavour which may be overcome by
the addition of a little lemon juice.
Try to make your own ice cream. I have given you two
recipes for this. One is suitable for everyday meals,
the other is much richer and is deliciously creamy, so
serve it to impress your friends on special occasions.
Colour and flavour balance is important when making
desserts. Tropical fruits have beautiful colours,
ranging from the pale gold of lime juice and bananas,
to the rich orange of mangoes and pawpaws.
These colours and flavours blend perfectly with berry
fruits such as strawberries and raspberries, with
delicious stone fruits such as peaches, nectarines and
apricots, and also with the fruits of the vine—grapes
and passionfruit.

Melon Ambrosia

Chilled fresh fruit or fruit salad is always an easy
dessert to serve in hot weather, but do try to give
it a little variety. Fruit creams, mousses
and soufflés are quite easy to make if you follow
the recipes carefully. They also look attractive and
have a rich, creamy, melt-in-the-mouth texture. They
may be made in advance so they are ideal to serve at
a dinner party.
Cool desserts need not be elaborate, but they should
be attractive and tempting to look at, as well as
delicious to eat. Serve them in simple dishes—
in well polished glass bowls or glazed china, or in
individual glasses which can be chilled in the
refrigerator—and you will serve them with pride.

Melon Fruit Cup

Serves 4–6

2 oranges
1½ cups seedless grapes
1½ cups diced melon
juice of 1 lemon
2 tablespoons sugar
fresh mint leaves for decoration, optional

Peel and section oranges, using a sharp serrated
knife. Place oranges in a bowl and add grapes, melon,
lemon juice and sugar. Mix lightly and chill.
Serve chilled, decorated with fresh mint if desired.

Lemon Cream Soufflé

Serves 6–8

3 eggs
$\frac{3}{4}$ cup castor sugar or powdered sugar
juice of 3 lemons
1 tablespoon gelatine
3 tablespoons hot water
$1\frac{1}{4}$ cups cream or chilled evaporated milk
2 tablespoons chopped nuts, $\frac{1}{2}$ cup extra cream
and 2 passionfruit or sliced fresh peach or segmented
mandarin for decoration

Secure a double piece of greaseproof paper or aluminium
foil around edge of a 2 pint soufflé dish, to come 3–4
inches above top of dish.
Place egg yolks, sugar and lemon juice in the top of
a double boiler, or in a heatproof bowl placed over a
saucepan of gently boiling water, and beat until mixture
thickens. Remove from heat, continue beating until
lukewarm.
Dissolve gelatine in 3 tablespoons hot water, stand aside
until lukewarm, then stir quickly in a thin continuous
stream into the egg yolk mixture. Both mixtures should
be at body temperature to combine correctly.
Whip cream until thick. Whisk egg white until stiff.
Fold cream and egg whites evenly into egg/lemon mixture,
pour into prepared soufflé dish and refrigerate until
set.
When set, remove band of paper and spoon chopped nuts
on to sides of soufflé. Decorate top edge with rosettes
of whipped cream and put passionfruit, peach or mandarin segments
in centre on top of soufflé.
Serve soufflé the same day it is made for best flavour
and texture.

97

Brandied Strawberries

Serves 6

3 cups strawberries
2 tablespoons icing sugar
6 tablespoons brandy or grand marnier

Place fresh strawberries in a bowl and sprinkle
with icing sugar and brandy. Leave to stand at
room temperature for at least 1 hour.
Serve in individual glasses, accompanied with thin
pouring cream if desired.

Ice Cream

Serves 12

1 × 20 oz can evaporated milk
1 teaspoon gelatine
1 tablespoon hot water
1 tablespoon sugar
2 tablespoons sherry
lemon or pink colouring, optional

Chill evaporated milk in refrigerator, overnight if
possible.
Dissolve gelatine in hot water. Whip evaporated milk
in a chilled mixing bowl until stiff. Stir in sherry
and cool dissolved gelatine. Add colouring to make a
pastel shade, if desired. Beat mixture for a further
minute and pour into two refrigerator trays. Place in
freezer to set.
Serve Ice Cream with fruit salad.
Variation: To make Cassata, add $\frac{1}{4}$ cup chopped cherries,
$\frac{1}{4}$ cup chopped almonds or walnuts and $\frac{1}{2}$ cup raisins to
mixture before freezing.

Banana Rum Mousse

Serves 6–8

1 packet lemon jelly (lemon jello)
1 cup mashed bananas
1 cup cream
2 tablespoons rum
extra whipped cream for serving

Make lemon jelly and chill until half set. Add mashed
bananas, whipped cream and rum and beat until smooth.
Pour into a serving dish and refrigerate until set.
Serve chilled, topped with whipped cream.

Banana Ice Cream

Serves 6–8

2 cups mashed bananas
$1\frac{1}{2}$ cups sugar
pinch of salt
$\frac{1}{2}$ cup pineapple juice
juice of 1 lemon
2 tablespoons rum
1 teaspoon powdered ginger
$1\frac{1}{4}$ cups cream

Mix together all ingredients, except cream, until
evenly combined. Whip cream and fold into mixture.
Place mixture in a refrigerator tray and place in
freezer until edges are mushy. Turn out into a
mixing bowl and beat until frothy. Return to refrigerator
tray and freeze until set.
Serve in chilled glasses.

Lemon Ice-Box Pie

Serves 10–12

2½ cups evaporated milk
1 cup wholemeal biscuit crumbs (graham cracker crumbs)
½ cup brown sugar
1 teaspoon nutmeg
1 teaspoon cinnamon
¼ teaspoon ground ginger
¼ teaspoon ground cloves
3 oz butter, melted
2 eggs
½ cup castor sugar or powdered sugar
grated rind and juice of 1 lemon
lemon jelly slices for decoration

Pour evaporated milk into a large freezing tray and
chill in freezer until icicles form.
Mix biscuit crumbs with brown sugar, spices and melted
butter until well combined. Press biscuit crumb mixture
over base of a large shallow cake tin or refrigerator
tray.
Separate eggs and mix egg yolks with castor sugar,
grated lemon rind and lemon juice. Whisk egg whites
until stiff and fold into egg yolk mixture.
Pour chilled evaporated milk into a large, chilled mixing
bowl and beat until thick. Fold carefully into egg
mixture. Pour into tray on top of spiced crumbs and
refrigerate until set.
To serve, cut into neat portions, and serve on individual
plates, decorated with segments of lemon jelly slices.

Fruits in Syrup

Serves 6–8

2 tablespoons sugar
4 tablespoons water
2 tablespoons dry sherry
2 teaspoons lemon or lime juice
$\frac{1}{2}$ teaspoon cinnamon
1 orange
2 cups fresh pineapple cubes
1 cup fresh mango or pawpaw cubes
$1\frac{1}{2}$ cups lychees

Dissolve sugar in water in a saucepan. Cool.
Stir in sherry, lemon juice and cinnamon.
Peel and segment orange neatly. Mix with remaining
fruit. Pour syrup over and chill for 1 hour.
Serve from chilled fruit bowl.
Note: If mango and pawpaw are unobtainable,
peaches or apricots may be substituted.

Melon Ambrosia

Serves 10–12

2 cups rock melon or canteloup balls or diced melon
2 cups honeydew melon balls or diced melon
2 oranges, peeled and sectioned
2 bananas, sliced
1 cup strawberries
$\frac{1}{2}$ cup green grapes
$\frac{1}{2}$ cup black or purple grapes
1 cup diced pawpaw or peach
4 tablespoons sugar
juice of 1 lemon
$\frac{1}{3}$ cup shredded coconut

Prepare fruit, mix with sugar and lemon juice and
chill. Serve topped with a sprinkling of coconut.
Note: Any colourful mixture of fruit may be added to the melon.

Three Fruit Sherbet

Serves 8

3 oranges
3 lemons
3 bananas
3 cups water
1–2 cups sugar
3 egg whites

Squeeze juice from oranges and lemons.
Mix bananas to a purée in a blender, or mash
well with a fork, then press through a sieve using
a wooden spoon.
Mix fruit juices and banana purée with water.
Add sugar to taste.
Pour into an ice tray and place in a freezer until
mixture is half frozen.
Remove from ice tray and fold in stiffly whisked
egg whites. Return to freezer until frozen.
Serve sherbet in chilled glasses.

Quick Orange Jelly/Jello

Serves 4–6

1 tablespoon gelatine
½ cup hot water
1¼ cups canned or fresh orange juice, chilled
6 crushed ice cubes

Dissolve gelatine in hot water.
Add chilled orange juice and stir in crushed
ice until ice melts.
Pour into a jelly mould, previously rinsed with
cold water, and refrigerate until set.
Serve jelly chilled with a fruit salad, cream or
ice cream, if desired.

Orange Creams

Serves 4

1 tablespoon gelatine
3 tablespoons hot water
2 cups canned or fresh orange juice, chilled
½ cup cream, whipped

Dissolve gelatine in hot water.
Add chilled orange juice and stir thoroughly.
Stir in whipped cream and pour into 4 individual
moulds, previously rinsed with cold water.
Stand moulds on ice tray and surround with ice.
Place in a freezer for 10–15 minutes or until
set.
Turn out and serve immediately or transfer to
food compartment of refrigerator until ready to
serve.

Oranges and Grapes Grand Marnier

Serves 6

6 oranges
8 oz green grapes
1 cup castor sugar or powdered sugar
$\frac{1}{2}$ cup water
juice of 1 lemon
6 tablespoons grand marnier
$\frac{1}{2}$ cup slivered almonds

Peel oranges with a sharp serrated knife. Take care
to remove all the rind and pith. Slice oranges across
thinly and place in a large bowl.
Wash, halve and deseed the grapes and add to sliced
oranges.
Place sugar and water in a saucepan and put over a
low heat. Stir until sugar is dissolved and bring
to the boil. Simmer for 1 minute, remove from heat,
add lemon juice and grand marnier.
Arrange oranges and grapes attractively in a serving
dish. Pour syrup over. Sprinkle with slivered almonds.
Chill well.
Serve with cream if desired.

Oranges and Grapes Grand Marnier

Grapefruit Mousse

Serves 6

2 eggs
$\frac{1}{2}$ cup castor sugar or powdered sugar
1 large grapefruit
1 tablespoon gelatine
3 tablespoons hot water
$1\frac{1}{4}$ cups cream
grapefruit segments for decoration

Separate eggs. Place egg yolks with castor sugar,
finely grated grapefruit rind and strained grapefruit
juice in the top of a double boiler. Beat over gently
bubbling water until mixture thickens. Cool.
Dissolve gelatine in hot water. Cool. Pour gelatine
into egg yolk mixture, in a steady stream, stirring
continuously. Both mixtures should be at body temperature
to combine correctly.
Whip cream until thick and whisk egg whites until stiff.
Fold into the egg/grapefruit mixture. Pour into a glass
serving bowl and refrigerate until set.
Serve chilled, decorated with grapefruit segments.

Orange Sorbet

Serves 4–6

¼ cup sugar
1¼ cups water
2 teaspoons gelatine
extra 2 tablespoons water
1 × 6 fl oz can concentrated orange juice
1 egg white

Place sugar and water in a saucepan and heat gently
until sugar dissolves. Cool.
Dissolve gelatine in 2 tablespoons water. Add to syrup.
Stir in orange juice. Pour into an ice tray and freeze
for 1 hour until about to set. Remove from freezer and
place in a bowl. Whisk egg white until stiff and fold
into orange mixture. Return to ice tray and freeze for
a further 2 hours before serving.
Serve in glasses.
Variation: A can of concentrated orange and passionfruit
juice may be used for a delicious flavoured sorbet.

Italian Lemon Water Ice

Serves 6

1¼ cups lemon juice (approx. 6 lemons)
1 cup sugar
2½ cups water
1 egg white, optional

Thinly pare the rind from 2 lemons. Squeeze the
juice from all the lemons.
Place sugar and water in a saucepan and heat gently
until sugar dissolves. Add lemon rind and boil gently
for 10 minutes. Leave to cool. Add the lemon juice
and strain into an ice-cube tray.
Place in the freezing compartment of the refrigerator
and leave until half frozen, about 1 hour. Turn mixture
into a bowl and fold in stiffly whisked egg white, if
desired. Return to ice-cube tray and re-freeze.
Serve in glasses or in the empty lemon caps. Cut a
slice from the bottom of each lemon cap before filling
with water ice, so that it will stand firmly.

Italian Lemon Water Ice (front)

Orange Souffle

Serves 6–8

3 eggs
1 cup castor sugar or powdered sugar
1 tablespoon gelatine
½ cup hot water
½ cup cold water
juice of 1 orange
juice of 1 lemon
pulp of 6 passionfruit
whipped cream for decoration

Separate eggs and whisk egg yolks with sugar in a
double boiler, over gently boiling water, until thick
and creamy.
Dissolve gelatine in hot water, stir in cold water.
Add fruit juices and passionfruit and stir well.
Mix egg yolk mixture with fruit juice mixture. Fold
in stiffly beaten egg whites until mixture has a smooth
consistency.
Pour mixture into a prepared soufflé dish (see page 97)
or into individual moulds, previously rinsed with cold
water. Chill in refrigerator until set.
Serve soufflé chilled decorated with whipped cream.
Note: The soufflé should be eaten the same day it is
prepared for best flavour and texture.

Mango Mousse

Serves 6

1 lb fresh mango pulp or canned mangoes (drained)
castor sugar or powdered sugar
1¼ cups cream
1 tablespoon gelatine
3 tablespoons orange or lemon juice

Mix mango pulp to a purée in a blender, or press
mangoes through a sieve with a wooden spoon. Make
purée up to 1½ cups with mango juice or water. Add
sugar to taste.
Whip cream and mix with the fruit purée until evenly
combined.
Dissolve gelatine in orange juice, cool. Stir dissolved
gelatine quickly into fruit mixture.
Pour mixture into a glass bowl and refrigerate until set.
Serve chilled.
Variation: Substitute pawpaw for mangoes to make a
Pawpaw Mousse. Alternatively, pulped canned or cooked
dried apricots can be used to make an Apricot Mousse.

Orange Souffle (page 114) and
Banana Rum Mousse (page 115)

Pineapple in Sour Cream

Serves 6

3 teaspoons gelatine
$\frac{1}{4}$ cup hot water
1 cup pineapple juice
1 cup chopped pineapple
1 cup sour cream
whipped cream for serving

Dissolve gelatine in hot water.
Add pineapple juice and chill in refrigerator until beginning to set.
Fold in chopped pineapple and sour cream.
Put mixture into 6 individual glasses and chill well until set.
Serve topped with whipped cream.

Iced Cream Cheese

Serves 6

8 oz cream cheese
1 cup cream
finely grated rind of 1 lemon
castor sugar or powdered sugar

Sieve cream cheese. Whip cream and mix with sieved
cheese until smooth. Add lemon rind and castor sugar
to taste.
Press mixture into a round container, previously lined
with muslin. Cover with aluminium foil and place in
freezer for 1–2 hours.
Turn out and serve with fresh berry fruit such as
strawberries, raspberries or red or black currants.

Cool Drinks

Sipping Cool Drinks is a pleasurably soothing hot
weather pastime. Cool Drinks are also good for you
because they quench the thirst and replace important
moisture lost in a hot climate.

I have given you some recipes for the ever popular
milkshake for children, refreshing iced coffee and
tea for adults, and long Cool Drinks and punches,
some alcoholic, some non-alcoholic.

Cool Drinks are instant refreshers in hot weather.
They are sure of a welcome at any summer party, for
they are good companions to cool food, refreshing
salads and spicy barbecues.

Fresh, citrus fruit drinks, with their sharp, tangy
flavour, are probably one of the most popular summer
thirst quenchers.

Cool alcoholic drinks are hot climate vitalizers.
Served chilled before a meal, they relax the mind
and stimulate the appetite; the meal to follow is
much more enjoyable.

Long Cool Drinks deserve tall, chilled, attractive
glasses. Chill the glasses in a refrigerator if
possible or with a special glass frosting gadget. If
the glasses are not chilled, add plenty of ice before
pouring in the drink, in order to serve it cold.

Colourful garnishes of sliced citrus fruit, oranges,
lemons and limes, cherries and strawberries and strips
of cucumber add a touch of sophistication to cool
drinks. They also give the party look that children
enjoy. So be a success this summer and serve Cool
Drinks with the professional touch.

Champagne and Orange Juice

Champagne and Orange Juice

For a festive occasion add chilled strained fresh orange juice to equal quantities of iced champagne.
Serve immediately.

Iced Orange

Serves 10

maraschino cherries
1 orange, sliced
½ bottle orange cordial
3 cups iced water
2 small bottles ginger ale

Make ice cubes with a cherry in the centre of each.
Place orange slices in a large chilled jug. Add orange cordial, iced water and ginger ale.
Serve chilled with ice cubes in each glass.

Orange Milk Shake

Serves 4

juice of 3 oranges
juice of 1 grapefruit
2 tablespoons sugar
2½ cups chilled milk

Mix all ingredients together in a blender.
Pour into tall glasses and serve immediately.

Wine Cooler

Serves 24

2 cups berry fruit, raspberries or cranberries
3 bananas, diced
2 cups chopped pineapple or 1 × 15 oz can
    pineapple pieces with juice
1 × 26 fl oz bottle lemonade
1 × 26 fl oz bottle rosé wine
1 × 26 fl oz bottle dry or sweet white wine

Mix berry fruit with bananas, pineapple and lemonade.
Chill well, overnight if possible.
Place ¼ cup fruit mixture in each tall glass. Add
ice cubes and fill glass with either rosé or white
wine.
Serve immediately with a tall spoon.

Sherry Refresher

Serves 4–6

juice of 3 grapefruit
½ cup dry or sweet sherry
soda water

Strain grapefruit juice into a jug.
Add sherry and chill well in refrigerator.
Serve chilled, 'topped up' with soda water to taste.

Iced Tea

Make a strong 'brew' of tea, cool and chill well.
Pour chilled tea into tall glasses over ice cubes
and serve with lemon wedges. Add a pinch of cinnamon
or mixed spice to each glass. Add sugar if desired.

Berry Milk Shake

Serves 6–8

2 cups ice cream
1 × 10 oz can raspberries
4 cups milk

Place all ingredients together in a blender and
mix until smoothly combined.
Serve in chilled glasses.

Cider Cup

Serves 10–12

$\frac{1}{2}$ cup mint leaves
2 × 26 fl oz bottles of cider
2 cups pineapple juice
2 large bottles ginger ale

Crush mint leaves and place in a large jug. Add cider
and pineapple juice. Chill well.
Serve chilled, 'topped up' with ginger ale.

Iced Coffee

Make some strong coffee using $1\frac{1}{2}$ teaspoons instant
coffee or 1 tablespoon ground coffee per person.
Cool and chill well.
Pour chilled coffee into tall glasses over ice cubes.
Serve topped with lighly whipped cream and grated chocolate.
Add sugar if desired.

Summer refreshers

Glossary

A glossary of terms used
in this book:

allspice
a mildly sharp and fragrant spice;
also known as pimento.

basil
an aromatic herb used in salads,
soups, stews and sauces;
excellent with tomato salads.

baste
to spoon liquid over food as
it cooks.

blanch
to pre-heat in boiling water
in order to whiten meats,
or to loosen skins of nuts or fruits.

bouillon
a clear soup, usually made
from beef.

bouillon cube
a soup or stock cube used to
flavour soups and stews.

capers
the flower buds of a
Mediterranean shrub; pickled,
they are used for garnishing and
flavouring.

caraway
aromatic seedlike fruit of a herb.

cayenne (red) pepper
the most pungent of spices,
hot and biting; can vary from hot
to extremely hot depending on
the blend used.

cinnamon
a powder made from the sweet,
spicy bark of the cinnamon tree.

cloves
a hot sweet spice with a highly
aromatic scent; may be used
whole or ground for pickling,
glazing ham and in some desserts.

consommé
a clear soup which has a light
gelatinous texture when cool.

coriander
a spice used in the making of
curry paste.

cream cottage cheese
a cottage cheese made from cream
rather than skim or whole milk.

cumin
a spice which is also an ingredient
of curry powder and curry paste.

filleting knife
a small, sharp, pointed,
steel knife, used to fillet fish,
meat and poultry; a smaller
version of the French kitchen knife.

garlic
a pungent bulb; used crushed or
finely chopped, to flavour meats
and salads.

gherkin
the young fruit of the cucumber;
pickled, it is used for garnishing
and for flavouring salads
and cold meats.

grand marnier
an orange-flavoured, brandy-
based liquer.

honeydew melon
a sweet-flavoured, white-fleshed
melon with a smooth, pale
green rind.

hors d'oeuvre
may be made up from meat,
fish, eggs, vegetables, salad or
fruit and from one or more
dishes; this term refers to the
appetizers served with cocktails
before sitting at the table;
hors d'oeuvres often form the
first course of the meal.

julienne
cut into fine strips about the size
of a matchstick.

ketchup
a thick, spicy, fruit sauce,
usually tomato-based; known as
'catsup' in some countries.

lychees
a small, soft, sweet, spicy fruit
with a fragile shell; available
in cans.

mace
the dried outer skin of the kernel
of the nutmeg; used in pickling
and in sweets and desserts.

maraschino cherries
cherries which are preserved and
bottled in maraschino; used to
decorate sweet dishes and
cool drinks.

marinade
a mixture of oil and an acid
such as vinegar, lemon juice
or wine, with the addition of
seasoning and flavourings;
used to 'marinate' or stand food in
for some time to give it more
flavour and to soften the tissues
of tough meat.

monosodium glutamate
a crystalline chemical product
added to food to bring out its
natural flavour; sometimes
called M.S.G. or accent.

oregano
a herb that is particularly good
with tomatoes and tomato sauces.

Parmesan
a hard, dry, strongly-flavoured
Italian cheese; usually finely
ground for cooking.

pawpaw or papaw
a fruit with rich orange flesh
grown in temperate and tropical
climates.

pot roaster
a flameproof, ovenproof casserole,
with a tight-fitting lid, in which
large joints of meat may be cooked
in the oven or on a hot plate.

125

port
a very sweet fortified red wine;
used to flavour desserts or as an
after dinner liquer.

rock melon
a sweet-flavoured light orange
melon with a rough brownish
skin; often known as cantaloup.

saffron
a spice made from the stamens of
the violet-coloured crocus,
used to colour food bright orange.

sake
a Japanese alcoholic drink
made from rice.

sambals
accompaniments which are
served with curry; these may be
hot, fruit chutneys or cool fruits
and vegetables dressed in French
dressing, lemon juice or yoghurt.

sauté
to fry lightly in a small amount of
fat or oil, turning frequently
during cooking.

scallops
a mollusc with a rounded
fluted-edged shell; used in
seafood dishes.

sesame seeds
seeds of a tropical herbaceous
plant; the small oval seeds have a
delicious flavour and can be
ground to obtain an oil.

shallots
long thin young onions, called
spring onions in some countries;
these are known as scallions in
US.

shred
to slice into thin strips.

sosatie
a Cape Malay (South African)
dish of curried meat, cooked in
small pieces on a skewer.

stock
liquid containing the flavour and
nutrients obtained from
prolonged boiling of bones,
meat, fish or vegetables.

tarragon
a herb native to Europe and
parts of Asia. It has a delicate,
aromatic flavour and is often used
in French dressing and other
classical French sauces.

turmeric
the ground stem or root of
a plant of the ginger family.

watercress
a dark green spray of leaves which
grows in fresh flowing streams
of water; used in salads and for
garnishing meat dishes.

zest
thinly-pared rind from citrus
fruit such as lemons, limes,
oranges and grapefruit.

zucchini or courgette
small green marrow-like
vegetable.

Index

127